INTO HIS PRESENCE

INTO HIS PRESENCE
The Lord's Prayer and the Tabernacle

H.L. ROBERTSON
Foreword by Dr. Dwain Miller

Into His Presence
Copyright © 2013 by H.L. Robertson. All rights reserved.

No part of this publication may be reproduced, stored in a retrieval system or transmitted in any way by any means, electronic, mechanical, photocopy, recording or otherwise without the prior permission of the author except as provided by USA copyright law.

Scripture quotations taken from the New American Standard Bible®, Copyright © 1960, 1962, 1963, 1968, 1971, 1972, 1973, 1975, 1977, 1995 by The Lockman Foundation. Used by permission.

Fairhaven Media, Lynchburg, TN

Cover design by Rtor Maghuyop
Interior design by Jomar Ouano

Published in the United States of America
ISBN: 978-0-9987-480-7-8

1. Religion / General
2. Religion / Biblical Studies / Old Testament
13.03.20

Dedication

To my beautiful wife who encouraged me to pursue this dream.

Foreword

Dr. Myles Munroe says, "There is no activity on earth more common than prayer. Every culture does it. However, there is no more frustrating, confusing, and suspicious area of human experience than prayer."

There has never been a more true statement than this one of Dr. Munroe. However, it is not enough to make generalizations as to the flaws and shortcomings of the prayer life of people around this God created globe. No, we must examine why in all of our efforts to pray, it seems that we are failing somehow in accomplishing the purpose of prayer.

Most people use prayer in order to gain something from the heavenly Father—blessings, favor, healing, protection, and provision are but a few of those main items on the prayer list of most believers. But is it not true that the Lord has already promised and provided those things to His children?

I submit to you that the reason the prayer life of most is ineffectual is because they are spending most of their time petitioning the heavenly Father for those things that He has already promised.

No, prayer is not the means whereby we obtain from the heavenly Father but rather the pathway into His presence. The major deficiency in the lives of the Father's people today is not a lack of prayer but a lack of His presence that releases them into the fullness of His purpose!

You are about to go on a journey *Into His Presence* that will forever change not only your view of prayer but your life. H.L. Robertson has masterfully unfolded the pathway into the presence of the Father by connecting the Lord's Prayer to the entrance of the holy of holies.

Get ready! This journey is what you have been looking for in your personal walk with the Father!

—Dr. Dwain Miler
Senior Pastor of Cross Life Church
El Dorado, Arkansas

Contents

Introduction 11
"Teach Us to Pray" 15
The Three Natures of Man 21
The Pattern of Worship 27
Our Father 33
Thy Kingdom Come 39
Thy Will Be Done 45
Give Us This Day 51
Forgive Us Our Debts 57
Lead Us Not 65
For Thine Is the Kingdom 71
Building the Tabernacle 79
Into His Gates 85
Appendix A 87
Appendix B 93

Introduction

> Behold, I stand at the door and knock; if anyone hears My voice and opens the door, I will come in to him, and will dine with him, and he with Me.
>
> Revelation 3:20

Even now the Son of God is standing and knocking at doors, both of individuals and of churches all over the world, seeking entrance to our hearts and lives. We are experiencing a season of visitation as described in Song of Solomon chapter 5:

> I was asleep, but my heart was awake. A voice! My beloved was knocking: "Open to me."
>
> Song of Solomon 5:2

Christ longs to come into an intimate relationship with his bride, his body, his church in these last days. We must learn to come into his manifest presence. The church has experienced this presence sporadically, at times not at all, in the past and falls far short of the model set out in the book of Acts. Even in the scripture quoted above, Christ is portrayed as being locked out of his own house by his bride. Only when it is too late and he has withdrawn does she realize what she has missed.

> I opened to my beloved, but my beloved had turned away and had gone!
>
> Song of Solomon 5:6

Scripture gives us a clear pattern for entering into his presence. We must identify it and apply it to our lives. Only then can we begin to see the church arise in her full potential as the apostle Paul says:

> Until we all attain…to the measure of the stature which belongs to the fullness of Christ.
>
> Ephesians 4:13

In the book of Acts, we see a church burgeoning with power. Why? Because it was a church composed of men and women who had experienced an encounter with Christ. Not just a meeting, but a personal encounter that forever changed their lives. These believers received spiritual power by having, not once, but on a continual basis, an intimate relationship with their Lord.

> In as much as many have undertaken to compile an account of the things accomplished among us, just as they were handed down to us by those who from the beginning were witnesses and servants of the word.
>
> Luke 1:1–2

In both the Old and New Testaments, those who have been eyewitnesses of the presence of the glory of the Lord have always come away indelibly marked by the event. The seal of God is evident in their lives and testimonies. A look at Jesus's lineage shows clearly the effects of the power of God. Murderers, idolaters, liars, cheats, and prostitutes grace his ancestry; unsavory characters transformed by a seeming chance meeting with the Lord. Many years ago, A. W. Tozer penned a classic devotional book entitled *The Pursuit of God*. It falls to each of us to "pursue God," to not only enter his presence, but to hover there as the cherubim covering the ark of the covenant did, to be transformed by the continuing power and presence of God in our daily walk:

> But we all, with unveiled face, beholding as in a mirror the glory of the Lord, are being transformed into the same image from glory to glory, just as from the Lord, the Spirit.
>
> 2 Corinthians 3:18

"Teach Us to Pray"

In the Old Testament, there was a definite pattern given for entering God's presence, for worship, for all things spiritual. We are told that the nation of Israel was to follow those patterns precisely as God had laid them out. We are also told that those things were merely "shadows" or representations of the true worship that God intends for us as the body of Christ to carry out.

> For every high priest is appointed to offer both gifts and sacrifices; so it is necessary that this high priest also have something to offer. Now if he were on earth, he would not be a priest at all, since there are those who offer the gifts according to the law; who serve a copy and shadow of the heavenly things, just as Moses was warned by God when he was about to erect the tabernacle; for, "See," He says, that you make all things according to the pattern which was shown you on the mountain.
>
> Hebrews 8:3–5

We are also told that these shadows and patterns are not to bring us into bondage to legalism, but we are to enter into the substance of the matter, which is Christ.

> Therefore no one is to act as your judge in regard to food and drink or in regard to a festival or a new moon or a Sabbath day—things which are a mere shadow of things to come; but the substance belongs to Christ.
>
> Colossians 2:16–17

In Luke 11:1, Jesus has a request from his disciples, "Teach us to pray." They aren't looking for magic words; they want a formula for approaching Almighty God in what is obviously a new and powerful spiritual economy. Jesus is making it clear that he, as Messiah, is fulfilling the law of Moses and that the status quo is not going to stand. His constant clashes with the Pharisees, Sadducees, and others in the Jewish religious establishment make that abundantly obvious. A new day has dawned spiritually, and the disciples have tasted enough of the heavenly dewdrops this bright new morning has produced to want more. Their heart cry is "how do we interact with the God of our fathers." In response, Jesus breathes what are most likely the most often repeated words ever spoken on this planet: the Lord's Prayer. Yet I believe they are far more than just a model prayer for them (not to mention us) to repeat. I believe they are an answer not just to the surface intent of the question they asked, but also a reply to the deeper questions within: How do we worship and approach a God who for countess centuries has been all but inapproachable to everyone but the priestly elite?

In the following chapters, we will walk through this prayer and use it to form a devotional pathway into a deeper and more intimate walk with our heavenly Father; a walk based on a daily, continuing encounter with his power and presence. The Old Testament pattern started at the gates of the tabernacle and culminated with an entrance into the holy of holies where the glory of God hovered over the ark of the covenant. Each step in between represents a step toward God and his awesome presence and power, not just a physical step but a spiritual step as well.

Jesus's model also takes us step by step from our daily lives, occupations, families, and cares into the presence of God. Each phrase resonates with a portion of tabernacle worship producing a pattern that we can each follow as individuals. We don't have to rely on an earthly high priest as the nation of Israel did, but we have a heavenly high priest who dwells within us and is eminently anxious to assist us in this spiritual discipline.

> This was in accordance with the eternal purpose which he carried out in Christ Jesus our Lord, in whom we have boldness and confident access though faith in him.
>
> Ephesians 3:11–12

> Since then we have a great high priest who has passed through the heavens, Jesus the Son of God, let us hold fast our confession. For we do not have a high priest who cannot sympathize with our weaknesses, but one who has been tempted in all things as we are, yet without sin. Therefore let us draw near with confidence to the throne of grace, so that we may receive mercy and find grace to help in time of need.
>
> Hebrews 4:14–16

Here we are told in Scripture that we can have "confident access." The King James Version renders Hebrews 4:16, "Come boldly before the throne of grace." This bold access comes not from irreverence but from a firmly rooted and unshakable confidence in our relationship with a loving heavenly Father. Romans chapter 8 says:

> For you have not been given a spirit of slavery leading to fear again, but you have received a spirit of adoption as sons by which you cry out, Abba! Father!
>
> Romans 8:15

We need a full, strong understanding that he wants us to approach him this way. We must have a mature knowledge, born in revelation from God's word, that he wants us to be in this kind of intimate family relationship with him. *Abba* is an Aramaic word meaning *papa*, a very loving intimate term. He desires us to not only come into but to spend time in and revel in his presence. In the following pages I want to lead you step by step through the pattern Jesus gave his disciples for entering into his presence, to teach you to spiritually journey through the tabernacle to arrive, finally, in the holy of holies with him!

> Do you not know that your body is a temple of the Holy Spirit who is in you.
>
> 1Corinthians 6:19

Lord, teach us to pray!

The Three Natures of Man

In understanding how man relates to God, we must first understand the nature of God and the nature of man. Genesis chapter 1 verses 26 and 27 tell us that we are made in God's image and in his likeness.

> Then God said, "Let Us make man in Our image, according to Our likeness"...God created man in His own image.
>
> Genesis 1:26–27

We must realize first of all that God has three natures and since man is made in God's image we also have three natures. God has revealed Himself to us as a Trinitarian being: God the Father, God the Word (the Son), and God the Holy Spirit.

> For there are three that bear record in heaven, the Father, the Word, and the Holy Ghost: and these three are one.
>
> 1 John 5:7, KJV

Man also is a three-part being having been made in God's image. In fact, Genesis chapter 2 shows us a picture of man's creation.

> Then the Lord formed man of the dust of the ground, and breathed into his nostrils the breath of life; and man became a living being.
>
> Genesis 2:7

In this narrative, we're shown man being formed from the earth (his body), having the breath of God imparted (his spirit), and his becoming a living soul. Just as the Father is the substance of God, the Word/Son is the expression of God and the Holy Spirit is the Spirit of God; the dust became the substance of man; man's living soul became the expression of man, and the spirit God breathed into him became the spirit of man. Man too is a Trinity, truly made in God's image.

Man has, first of all, an external nature, which Scripture calls the flesh, the outward man, or the body. Secondly man has an internal nature which consists of the soulish realm—the mind, will, and emotions. It is what the Bible calls the heart or the inward man. Thirdly, man has an eternal nature, which is called the breath or the spirit of man.

> For I know that nothing good dwells in me, that is, in my flesh; for the willing is present in me, but the doing of good is not.…I find the principle that evil is present in me, the one who wishes to do good. For I joyfully concur with the law of God in the inner man, but I see a different law in the members of my body.
>
> Romans 7:18–23

> Therefore we do not lose heart, but though our outer man is decaying, yet our inner man is being renewed day by day.
>
> 2 Corinthians 4:16

Before an individual reaches what theologians commonly call the "age of accountability," their body is alive but slowly dying, and their spirit and soul are alive. Sin is present in the flesh through the fall of Adam; however, no sin is imputed or charged to their account, and they live in innocence of sin.

> The Law brings about wrath, but where there is no Law, neither is there violation.
>
> Romans 4:15

After they reach the age of accountability and the knowledge of sin, their body is still alive but slowly dying, their soul is condemned, and their spirit is dead.

> I was alive apart from the Law; but when the commandment came, sin became alive and I died.
>
> Romans 7:9

After the individual comes to salvation in Jesus Christ, the body continues to be alive but slowly dying, the soul is still in an alive, but fallen, state in need of renewing, and the spirit has been resurrected and sealed. Although sin is still present in the individual's life, it is not charged to their account, and instead, Christ's righteousness is credited to them.

> Therefore, there is now no condemnation for those who are in Christ Jesus.
>
> Romans 8:1

So what's the final outcome?

> Then the dust will return to the earth as it was, and the spirit will return to God who gave it.
>
> Ecclesiastes 12:7

The soul then goes to its eternal destiny based on our decision to believe or not believe in Jesus Christ.

Now we have examined the three natures of God, and we have also examined the three natures of man; man who was made in his image and likeness. Is it any surprise to us to find that the tabernacle of Moses, which was man's first vehicle or system we might say, to approach and worship God would also be a three-part structure? This structure was in fact arranged in exact accordance to the pattern we see in the three natures of man. We see an outer court, which corresponds to the external nature or body of man; we see in the inner court, the holy place, which corresponds with the internal nature, the soul of man; and we also see the holy of holies or innermost court, which corresponds with the eternal nature of man or the spirit of man.

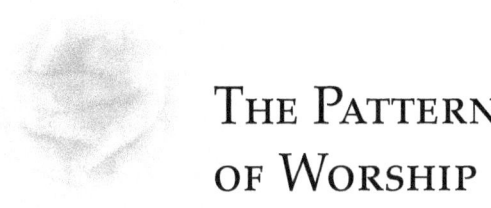

The Pattern of Worship

I would like to introduce to you the Old Testament pattern of worship; the pattern that was given to Moses on Mount Sinai. It was, however, given to him only after the children of Israel had rejected God's personal presence, authority, and relationship. This pattern centered around what is known as the tabernacle of Moses. The description of this tabernacle was found in Exodus chapters 25 through 27.

First of all, we find that the tabernacle was surrounded by a wall. This wall separated the inner workings of the tabernacle and the worship experience, which was guided by the priests, from the outside world, sanctifying it and keeping it separate from the day-to-day activities. In this wall was a single pair of gates facing due east. The fact that an individual had to enter in by this set of gates signified the concept that it took a conscious decision and effort to separate oneself from his day-to-day activities and to enter into a place of worshiping the

Almighty. The space inside the gates was known as the outer court. Any Israelite could enter here and bring his sacrifice and/or offering to the priests to be offered to God.

This outer court corresponds to the body, the physical realm, the external nature of man. It was here that the most basic level of worship and sacrifice began. The item to be sacrificed or offered to the Lord was then given to the priests who carried out the appropriate ceremony to offer it to God. Contained inside the enclosure were the great altar and the bronze laver with the laver just inside the gate and the altar behind it in a direct line toward the door of the holy place.

The first item in the tabernacle was the great altar of sacrifice. The altar sat directly inside the gates of the tabernacle. It was on this altar that the offerings and sacrifices were made by the priests and a fire was kept continually burning here. It was here that all the burnt offerings, all the drink offerings, and all the wave offerings were made. During feast times, there were literally thousands of sacrifices a day made on the altar. These sacrifices represented offerings for sin, thanksgiving, first fruits, and many other specific purposes.

> And you shall make the altar of Acacia wood, five cubits long and five cubits wide; the altar shall be square, and its height shall be three cubits. You shall make its horns on its four corners; its horns shall be one piece with it, and you shall overlay it with bronze.
>
> Exodus 27:1–2

The second piece of furniture, and therefore, the second step in the process of worship was the laver, also known as the brazen sea (KJV). This was, in fact, a huge washing vessel in which the priests would ceremonially wash and cleanse themselves before beginning the actual acts of sacrifice before the Lord. Ritual washing and cleansing were an integral part of the Jewish ceremonial liturgy.

> You shall also make a bronze laver, with its base of bronze, for washing; and you shall put it between the tent of meeting and the altar, and you shall put water in it. Aaron and his sons shall wash their hands and feet from it; when they shall enter the tent of the meeting they shall wash with water, that they may not die; or when they approach to the altar to minister, offering up in smoke and the fire sacrifice to the Lord.
>
> Exodus 30:18–20

The next section of the tabernacle was a tentlike structure called the holy place or the inner court. Only the priests were allowed to enter this section of the tabernacle. This tent was entered by a door, again facing due east. Inside this tent were three more pieces of the tabernacle furniture. These were the table of shewbread, the golden lampstand or menorah, and the golden altar of incense.

On the right-hand or north side as you entered was a table of shewbread. This is the medium-size table on which the hallowed bread was placed before the Lord.

> You shall make a table of acacia wood, two cubits long and one cubit wide and one and a half cubits high. You shall overlay it with pure gold and make a gold border around It...You shall set the bread of the presence on the table before me at all times.
>
> Exodus 25:23–24, 30

On the south or left hand side of the holy place opposite the table was the menorah. The seven-branched golden lampstand that was perpetually kept lit to represent the continual presence of the Spirit of God in the tabernacle.

> Then you shall make a lampstand of pure gold. The lampstand and its base and its shaft are to be made of hammered work; its cups, its bulbs, and its flowers shall be one piece with it.
>
> Exodus 25:31

Directly in line with the door, on the western wall of the holy place, was the golden altar of incense. This was a tall slender table on which coals of fire were placed from the great altar outside and on which incense was burned. It was here that the high priest offered the holy incense morning and evening and just before entering the holy of holies.

> Moreover, you shall make an altar as a place for burning incense; you shall make it of acacia wood. Its length shall be a cubit, and its width a cubic, it shall be square, and its height shall be two cubits; is horns shall be of one piece with it.
>
> Exodus 30:1–2

Directly behind the altar of incense was a veil. This veil was seamless and had no opening in it. Access into the holy of holies beyond was gained by crawling under the veil. This was done only once per year when the high priest entered to make the atonement offering for the sins of the whole nation. Inside the veil was the ark of the covenant. This was a gold-covered wooden box that contained the sacred pieces of the covenant: the stone tablets with the Ten Commandments that were given to Moses on Mount Sinai, Aaron's rod or walking staff that had budded, and a golden pot containing manna that had been collected while the nation of Israel had wandered in the wilderness. The covering for this box, which was also called the mercy seat or the place of atonement, was decorated with two large golden cherubim whose wings were extended forward so that they touched or almost touched in the middle of the covering.

> They shall construct an ark of acacia wood two and a half cubits long, and one and a half cubits wide, and one and a half cubits high. You shall overlay it

with pure gold, and inside and out you shall overlay it, and you shall make a gold molding around it... You shall make two cherubim of gold, make them of hammered work at the two ends of the mercy seat. Make one cherub at one end and one cherub at the other end; you shall make the cherubim of one piece with the mercy seat at its two ends. The cherubim shall have their wings spread upward, covering the mercy seat with their wings and facing one another; the faces of the cherubim are to be turned toward the mercy seat. You shall put the mercy seat on top of the ark, and in the Ark you shall put the testimony which I shall give you. There I will meet with you; and from above the mercy seat, between the two cherubim which are upon Ark of the testimony, I will speak to you.

Exodus 25:10–11, 18–22

God considered this piece of furniture so holy that even to touch it was instant death for any person, even the priests. When being transported, it was carried by the priests on long poles run through rings on its side to accommodate this restriction. The Ark with the mercy seat, or place of atonement, was the focal point of the entire tabernacle worship system. It was here, as verse 22 tells us, that God promised to meet with the high priest, commune with him, and communicate with them. This was truly the heart of Old Testament worship and interaction with God.

Our Father

Before teaching his disciples to pray, Jesus taught them how to prepare to pray. In Matthew 6:6 he said:

> But you, when you pray, go into your inner room, close your door and pray to your Father who is in secret, and your Father who sees what is done in secret will reward you.
>
> Matthew 6:6

Notice that he didn't say, "Your Father who hears in secret," but "who sees in secret." God looks not just at our words, but at our actions and at our inner thoughts and intents. He wants us to set our hearts and minds on him. He wants us to shut out the world and shut ourselves in! He is teaching us to establish a quiet place and time to enter into his presence, our "inner room." The psalm says:

> He who dwells in the shelter of the Most High Will
> abide in the shadow of the Almighty.
>
> Psalm 91:1

The word *shelter* here means the secret place or hidden place. This indicates to us that the place of our meeting with God is not only a place of shelter but a place for protection as well. This place comprises not only the journey, but also the object of that journey in our quest to seek God's presence. Notice also that he says, "He who dwells." This indicates his firm intention that this is a spiritual discipline that is an ongoing, regular practice. The very first step in the journey involves entering into the gates of the tabernacle spiritually. Psalms 100 says that we are to:

> Enter his gates with thanksgiving and his courts with praise.
>
> Psalm 100:4

We see in this verse the words *thanksgiving* and *praise*. This shows the importance of worship in this entering-in process, and we get the first inkling that the idea of worship is going to be sprinkled throughout. In fact, many people find it helpful to have worship music playing softly in the background during their prayer and communion time with the Lord. This not only enhances the process of entering the gates with thanksgiving and praise but also provides a suitable spiritual atmosphere to begin this time. On the other hand, there may and probably will come a point at which it is desirable to "be still" before the Lord in total silence.

> Pray, then in this way: Our Father who is in heaven, Hallowed be Your name.
>
> Matthew 6:9

Here in this first portion of the Lord's Prayer, Jesus is teaching us the principle that we must honor and praise God as we begin to approach His presence. We must understand and acknowledge his Lordship, his power, and the all-important fact that he is a loving Father who wants to receive us.

Entering the gates of the tabernacle places the worshiper in the outer court of the structure. This corresponds to our outer court: the body or the external nature. It is here that we encounter the first two pieces of the tabernacle furniture, the great altar and the bronze laver. The worshiper entering the tabernacle presents the offering to the priests to be sacrificed on the altar. However, we, who the Scriptures call priest and kings, approach the tabernacle furniture in the way that the priests would have in the time of Moses, i.e., we will approach the laver first for the ceremonial cleansing, followed by coming to the altar to offer our spiritual sacrifices.

> And He has made us to be a kingdom, priests to His God and Father.
>
> Revelation 1:6

> But you are a chosen race, a royal Priesthood.
>
> 1 Peter 2:9

These verses point out our position in the kingdom of God as priesthood of believers, dependent only on our own desire to serve and his guidance to minister for and before the Lord.

Prayer for entrance into the tabernacle:

Our Father who is in heaven, Hallowed be Your name. I enter the tabernacle of your presence with thankfulness. Thank you for your many and great blessings. Thank you for your free gift of salvation in your Son, Jesus Christ. For all your supply and blessings, which were accomplished and provided by the finished work of the cross. I thank you, and I praise you. I magnify and declare holy your great name, for you are worthy of all worship and honor and glory and power and blessing and praise forever. In Jesus's name, amen.

Life challenge:

It is important to enter his presence in this close personal way—free from distractions. What do you need to lay aside as you come into his courts? What mental tapes, playing in your head, that keep you from concentrating on him, do you need to turn off?

Thy Kingdom Come

The next phrase of the Lord's Prayer, "Your kingdom come" is born of a desire for cleansing and purification. It is a cry for Christ to be enthroned in the believer's heart ("your kingdom"). Self must be deposed and Christ exalted in his place, allowing the Holy Spirit to wash away the "stuff" of the outside world that attaches itself to each one of us.

In Bible times, upon entering any home, it was customary to have one's feet washed. Sharing the dusty streets and roads with countless animals caused a person's feet to be seriously defiled and unclean. It was considered absolutely necessary to cleanse oneself when entering someone's house. How much more then was it necessary to do so when entering God's house! The priests were also supposed to wash their hands. You see, it's not just what of the world that touches you, but it's also what of the world you touch that must be dealt with.

> You shall make a laver of bronze, with its base of bronze, for washing...Aaron and his sons shall wash their hands and their feet from it; when they enter the tent of meeting, they shall wash with water, that they may not die; or when they approach the altar to minister.
>
> Exodus 30:18–20

As you can see from this passage, for Aaron's sons, the priests to minister in the tabernacle without properly cleansing themselves ceremonially at the bronze laver was so serious an offense that they could actually be killed by the Lord for this infraction. It was essential for them to purge themselves from the world and its influences before ministering. In fact, Exodus 40:11 says that the laver itself had to be anointed and consecrated before the priests washed themselves. This concept of consecration—a religious and spiritual separation—is carried consistently throughout the Old Testament. This is the precise purpose for the cleansing at the laver, a ceremonial separation from the world outside. In Luke 16, Jesus says,

> No servant can serve two masters...You cannot serve God and Mammon [the world system].
>
> Luke 16:13

For us as believers, the implication is plain: if we do not separate and cleanse ourselves of worldly thoughts and influences before attempting to enter God's presence, we are still, in our hearts and minds, serving the world system. Ephesians tells us:

> Christ...loved the church and gave Himself up for her, so that He might sanctify her, having cleansed her by the washing of water with the word.
>
> Ephesians 5:26

Here we are shown a word picture of Christ sanctifying (cleansing and setting apart) the church, i.e., the body of His believers by His word.

As I pointed out in the last chapter, notice that for the individual worshiper beginning his approach to God, the altar was the first station. However, for the priests who minister before the Lord, the laver was the first stop. This speaks to the fact that to come to the Lord for salvation the individual comes "just as I am"; but to go farther in the relationship and begin to minister and enter into the Lord's service, one must begin that process of cleansing and sanctification.

Even the bronze for the making of the laver connects to the concept of consecration from self and from the world. Exodus 38:8 tells us that the laver was made from bronze mirrors belonging to the women who served at the door of the tabernacle. The articles that we as human beings use to groom and admire ourselves were used by God as the raw materials to create a vessel for cleansing us from that very human centeredness. This also points up the fact that God sees us in a vastly different way than we see ourselves.

> For God sees not as man sees, for man looks at the outward appearance, but the Lord looks at the heart.
>
> 1 Samuel 16:7

As you enter into this portion of approaching God, just imagine that huge bronze vessel filled with water, pointing skyward, pointing to God. Imagine yourself as that priest walking up to the laver and sending a reflection of yourself heavenward. You're not sending just a physical reflection but an inward heart scan. With his life potentially on the line, we can only assume that the priest took his washing very seriously. How much more so should we as believers take this to heart when we consider that we have the Holy Spirit living inside us!

Prayer for cleansing at the laver:

Heavenly Father, your kingdom come in my life, in my will, in my attitudes, and in my behavior. Cleanse me of all sins, worldly distractions, and thoughts patterns. Create in me a clean heart and a mind centered on you alone as I come into this time of prayer and fellowship with you. Sanctify me as a vessel fit for your service and worship. In Jesus's name, amen.

Life challenge:

Just as ceremonial, physical cleansing was an important step in tabernacle worship, mental and emotional cleansing is crucial for us as we enter in. What worldly or even ungodly thoughts and thought patterns do you need to let him cleanse as you come into his presence?

Thy Will Be Done

After cleansing and purifying themselves at the laver, the priests were clothed in their priestly garments and consecrated by the burnt offering of a young bull followed by several various offerings to the Lord. They would then begin to carry out their appointed functions in the tabernacle. The primary function in this regard for most of the priests (other than the high priest) would be to make sacrifices, both for themselves and for the people as they came to worship.

Exodus 27:5 tells us that the altar had a raised ledge (or "compass," depending on the translation.) This ledge was a raised platform on which the priests stood to conduct the sacrifices, but there were no steps. The obvious symbolic implication of the fact that there were no steps is that while we must make the effort to approach God, it is not by works (steps) that we come to Him. Exodus 20:26 says that it should have no steps so that the priests' "nakedness" would not be exposed as they ascended the platform. In fact, Exodus 20:42

tells us that the priests were to wear linen breeches from their loins to their thighs to cover themselves for this very reason. These breeches resonate with the fact that we need the covering of Christ's righteousness to make this approach to God.

Three main types of offerings were made here at the altar: burnt offerings, drink offerings, and wave offerings. Just as the animals set forth as burnt offerings were totally consumed by the fire, we must be totally consumed in His worship. Secondly, we must also be willing to be poured out like the drink offerings in His service. Finally, we need to submit to be like the wave offering, which was waved before the Lord, passed through the smoke of the altar, and then used as provision for the priests and their families. This is a symbolic picture of our mandate to give selflessly of time and our substance to the Lord's service. "Your will be done" is a sacrifice of self and self-will on the altar of sacrifice before God. It represents a total consecration of yourself to Him.

> Therefore I urge you brethren, by the mercies of God to present your bodies a living and holy sacrifice, acceptable to God, which is your spiritual act of worship. And do not be conformed to this world, but be transformed by the renewing of your mind.
>
> Romans 12:1–2

The breaking of self-will brings first submission and then obedience. King David describes the breaking of self in Psalm 51:

> For you do not delight in sacrifice, otherwise I would give it; you are not pleased with burnt offering. The sacrifices of God are a broken spirit; A broken and a contrite heart, O God, you will not despise.
>
> Psalms 51:16–17

Even self-willed actions that are born of religious fervor are equated to rebellion by God. King Saul learned this bitter lesson by taking animals from what God clearly said was dedicated to himself, ostensibly to make sacrifices to the Lord.

> Samuel said, Has the Lord as much delight in burnt offerings and sacrifices As in obeying the voice of the Lord? Behold, to obey is better than sacrifice, And to heed than the fat of rams.
>
> 1 Samuel 15:22

God makes it clear that, without obedience to His commands, outward religious ceremony is not only empty of meaning, but it is an offense to Him. In fact, this principle extends to all phases of our Christian walk. Hosea 6:6 says:

> For I delight in loyalty rather than sacrifice, And in knowledge of God rather than burnt offerings.
>
> Hosea 6:6

Jesus quoted the Greek Septuagint translation of this verse in Matthew 9:13 when confronting a group of Pharisees about their blatant twisting of the law to put emphasis on outward appearances and characteristics to the detriment of the people and their own ministry.

> Go and learn what this means: "I desire compassion and not sacrifice," for I did not come to call the righteous, but sinners to repentance.
>
> Matthew 9:13

Everything we do or intend to do must pass through the flames of that altar and be tried by the fire of His judgment. God desires for us to operate as Jesus did:

> Truly, truly I say to you, the Son can do nothing of Himself, unless it is something He sees the Father doing; for whatever the Father does, these things the Son also does in like manner. For the Father loves the Son, and shows Him all things that He Himself is doing...I can do nothing on my own initiative.
>
> John 5:19–20, 30

Prayer for cleansing at the altar:

Father, "Your will be done" in every part of my life, my thought processes, my attitudes, and my Christian walk. Right now, by an act of my will, I lay myself on your altar as a living sacrifice. I crucify my flesh according to Galatians 2:20 that no longer will it be me that lives, but Christ who lives in me. I put myself in submission to your will and in obedience to your word so that I can worship you and serve others. Prepare me to enter into your holy place. In Jesus's name, amen.

Life challenge:

Throughout the New Testament we are taught to live a crucified life, a life that places self and self-will on the altar of sacrifice to his will. What areas of your life do you struggle with submitting to him? When is the temptation greatest for self to "crawl off the altar" and retake control of your life?

Give Us This Day

Upon completing ministry at the great altar, certain priests would then enter the holy place or "tent of meeting." They entered by way of the door into a tent chamber that, as previously described, contained the table of shewbread or bread of the presence, the menorah, and the altar of incense. Only when an individual has been cleansed of the world and stripped of self can they truly be ready to enter the inner court, a place of deeper communion with God. Notice also, that like the priests in Moses's time, this must be a continuing day-by-day process. This process of cleansing and self-denial, when carried out as a regular spiritual discipline, will result in a deep-seeded purification and an ever-closer relationship with the Lord.

The actual table and its implements are greatly symbolic of our relationship and communion with God. Exodus chapter 25 describes these vessels on the table.

> You shall make its dishes and its pans and its jars and its bowls with which to pour drink offerings; you shall make them of pure gold. You shall set the bread of the Presence on the table before me at all times.
>
> Exodus 25:29–30

Leviticus chapter 24 further describes the actual ministry at the table of the bread.

> Then you shall take fine flour and bake twelve cakes with it; two-tenths of an ephah shall be in each cake. You shall set them into rows, six in a row, on the pure gold table before the Lord. You shall put pure frankincense on each row that it may be a memorial portion for the bread, even an offering by fire to the Lord. Every Sabbath day he shall set it in order before the Lord continually; it is an everlasting covenant for the sons of Israel. It shall be for Aaron and his sons and they shall eat it in the holy place for it is most holy to him from the Lord's offering by fires, his portion forever.
>
> Leviticus 24:5–9

The ordering of the items on the table of bread is as follows: the loaves of bread were placed in stacks of six into pans. There was then a lid placed on the pans. On top of this was placed a small cuplike container, which would contain a lump of pure frankincense. Next to these sat two bowls of wine. The bread, frankincense, and wine were placed on the table of the bread each Sabbath day. They remained there all week, and on the following Sabbath day, the priests replaced them with fresh articles following which the bread and wine were consumed by the priests and the frankincense was burned on the altar.

The twelve loaves represented each of the twelve tribes of the nation of Israel. The fact that each tribe was represented by a separate loaf is symbolic of the all-inclusiveness of God's plan. The two stacks represent the invitation to both Jew and Gentile to God's table of provision; salvation is available to all through Jesus's sacrifice. This arrangement also speaks to the fact that the entering of the holy place is something that is available to each believer; all were included. The presence of the bread continually before the Lord on the table is symbolic of the fact that our presence in fellowship and communion with God is to be a continual, ongoing endeavor, not just a weekly visit. Although the priests went in to replace the bread once a week on the Sabbath, the bread was there perpetually.

The frankincense is symbolic of the idea that our times of presence before the Lord should be seasoned with praise and worship. The frankincense was a key ingredient of the incense of the altar that was burned before the Lord (Exodus 30:34). As I outlined in chapter 4, a proper attitude of praise, worship, and thanksgiving is an essential thread throughout the tabernacle worship experience. In the Old Testament, the Lord repeatedly speaks of the concept of soothing aromas rising up before him from sacrifices and from the incense.

The presence of the wine in conjunction with the bread indicates to us that this is to be a time of close fellowship. The fact that the bread was not unleavened separates this concept from the practice of the Passover supper and its New Testament counterpart in the Lord's supper. In the cultures of the Bible, sharing a meal together is considered one of the most intimate acts of fellowship that people can have; a tradition which has been carried over in Middle Eastern cultures even to the present time. The weekly eating of the bread by the priests also points out to us the importance of regular fellowship with other believers.

The crux of this step in the tabernacle journey is to show the need for not only daily time spent with God in prayer and Bible study (the bread of life) but continual fellowship with Him. This, again, must be compounded with praise and worship, just as the frankincense was mingled with spices in the holy incense.

> It is written, Man shall live on bread alone, but on every word that proceeds out of the mouth of God.
>
> Matthew 4:4

Prayer for abiding at the table of bread:

Lord, Give me this day my daily bread, the bread of life that comes only from you. Help me to be in a perpetual state of prayer and meditation on you and your word. Create in me a thankful heart that is always set on praising and worshipping you. Change me in your glorious presence. In Jesus's name, amen.

Life challenge:

The spiritual disciplines of Bible reading/study, prayer, and communion with God are all vitally important in the life of a believer. In which of these areas do you sense God pointing out to you a deficiency in your daily walk?

Forgive Us Our Debts

The second article of furniture in the holy place was the menorah or lampstand. This seven-branched lamp was fueled by pure beaten olive oil.

> You shall charge the sons of Israel, that they bring you clear oil of beaten olives for the light, to make a lamp burn continually. In the tent of meeting outside the veil which is before the testimony, Aaron and his sons shall keep it in order from evening to morning before the LORD; it shall be a perpetual statute throughout their generations for the sons of Israel.
>
> Exodus 27:20–21

The menorah was the source of light for the holy place. Its continual flame and light represented the presence and illumination of the Holy Spirit. The picture of the seven branches and their corresponding lamp bowls is referenced in the New Testament to signify the presence of the Spirit in the seven great New Testament churches in Asia Minor as shown in Revelation chapters 1–3. These churches were an "everyman" of church life, each representing both a type of church and a period in church history.

> John to the seven churches that are in Asia: Grace to you and peace, from Him who is to come, and from the seven Spirits who are before His throne...Then I turned to see the voice that was speaking to me. And having turned I saw seven golden lampstands; and in the middle of the lampstands I saw one like a son of man, clothed in a robe reaching to the feet, and girded across His chest with a golden sash.
>
> Revelation 1:4, 12–13

> To the angel of the church in Ephesus write: The One who holds the seven stars in His right hand, the One who walks among the seven golden lampstands...Therefore remember from where you have fallen, and repent and do the deeds you did at first; or else I am coming to you and will remove your lampstand out of its place—unless you repent.
>
> Revelation 2:1, 5

He obviously is referring to the presence of the Holy Spirit in this threatened judgment for the unrepentant church. Just as the menorah represented the Holy Spirit in the tabernacle and the seven lampstands represented the Spirit's presence in the seven churches in Asia, we can see the symbolic picture of his presence indwelling our "tabernacle." Romans says:

> However, you are not in the flesh but in the Spirit, if indeed the Spirit of God dwells in you. But, if anyone does not have the Spirit of Christ, he does not belong to Him.
>
> Romans 8:9

This clearly shows us that as true believers in Christ we have the Holy Spirit dwelling within us. In the same way that the menorah provided light to the holy place for the priests to minister, the Holy Spirit living within us provides illumination to our lives. He shines the light of truth on the hidden recesses of our hearts to bring to view those areas that need God's hand upon to make changes and adjustments. Scripture shows us this principle numerous times:

> The Spirit of man is the lamp of the LORD, Searching all the innermost parts of his being.
>
> Proverbs 20:27

> For the word of God is living and active and sharper than any two-edged sword, and piercing as far as the division of soul and spirit, of both joints

and marrow, and able to judge the thoughts and intentions of the heart.

> Hebrews 4:12

The central theme of this part of the Lord's Prayer, "Forgive us our debts, as we also have forgiven our debtors," is a petition asking God to give us forgiveness and cleansing as we practice forgiveness. He goes on in the verses following the prayer to add:

> For if we forgive others for their transgressions, your heavenly Father will also forgive you. But if you do not forgive others, then your Father will not forgive your transgressions.
>
> Matthew 6:14–15

In Matthew 18:23–34, Jesus teaches the parable of the unjust servant, in which a servant is forgiven a huge debt by his master only to have his fellow servant thrown into prison for a much, much smaller debt. He was then thrown into prison himself for his hardness of heart and Jesus says at the end of the parables:

> My heavenly Father will also do the same to you, if each of you does not forgive his brother from your heart.
>
> Matthew 18:35

The point of this parable is that we, who are forgiven our sin debt, should forgive our brothers and sisters in Christ. If we refuse this forgiveness, we will not be forgiven by God. It is absolutely necessary to have a clean heart, free of unforgiveness before we approach the altar. Jesus introduced to us this principle in Mark chapter 11:

> Therefore I say to you, all things for which you pray and ask, believe that you have received them, and they will be granted you. Whenever you *stand praying* [emphasis mine], forgive, if you have anything against anyone, so that your Father who is in heaven will also forgive your transgressions. But if you do not forgive, neither will your Father who is in heaven forgive your transgressions.
>
> Mark 11:24–26

He elaborated on it in Matthew chapter 5:

> But I say to you that everyone who is angry with his brother shall be guilty before the court … Therefore if you are presenting your offering at the altar, and there remember that your brother has something against you, leave your offering there before the *altar* [emphasis mine] and go, first be reconciled to your brother, and then come and present your offering.
>
> Matthew 5:22–24

We also see it in this passage a prayer to bring us out from all lifestyles and attitudes that are not of him. We plead with him for that illumination to be shined into our hearts to show us clearly where we need his help giving forgiveness to others.

> Search me, O God, and know my heart; Try me and know my anxious thoughts; And see if there be any hurtful way in me, And lead me in the everlasting way.
>
> Psalm 139:23–24

The cleansing process is never ending for the believer. The menorah had to be tended twice daily, wicks trimmed and eventually replaced, oil bowls filled, and soot and impurities cleaned away. In the same way we as believers have to undergo this "tending" process. Romans 12:2 says we are to be transformed by the renewing of our minds. Transformation is exactly that, a process, not an event. Is it any wonder then that scripture says we are to "pray without ceasing" (1 Thessalonians 5:17)?

Ephesians 5:18 commands us to be filled with the Spirit. The tense of the Greek verb here is a historical present, which implies an ongoing action. The reason? We leak! We, as believers, are still trapped in fallen, fallible human bodies and need this continual infilling and transformation under the scrutinizing gaze of God's light. The mood of the Greek verb here is imperative. This is a command, an absolutely essential, not only act but daily spiritual discipline. We need to be cleansed and filled to prepare to approach the altar of incense; the last stop before entering the holy of holies.

Prayer for standing before the menorah:

Father God, I come to you with open arms and heart. I stand before the light of your word and invite you to search me and try me. Show me the areas of my life, attitudes, actions, and thought processes that don't meet your standard. Forgive me my debts, my sins against you. Give me strength so that I, by an act of my will, can give forgiveness. Purge out of me everything that hinders our fellowship so that your light can shine through me more clearly in a dark and fallen world. In Jesus's name, amen.

Life challenge:

As believers we are spiritually illuminated by the Holy Spirit living within us. However, it is also fundamental to our Christian walk to exhibit the fruit of the Spirit and to operate in the power of the Holy Spirit. Which of the fruits of the Spirit listed in Galatians 5:22-23 do you demonstrate the most? The least? Do you pray regularly (or ever) for the filling and empowerment of the Holy Spirit?

Lead Us Not

The final piece of furniture in the holy place was the altar of incense. As previously described, it was an altar made of acacia wood covered with gold and used to burn the holy incense. This incense was made of equal parts of stacte, a sweet spice probably derived from the storax tree; onycha, a strong scent made from ground mussel shells; galbanum, a strong, disagreeable-smelling aromatic gum; and frankincense, a fragrant gum made from the Boswellia tree. These ingredients combined to produce formidable incense which was, no doubt, a "soothing aroma" to the Lord; the words "soothing aroma" are used some thirty-nine times in the Torah alone to describe offerings made to the Lord.

> You shall put this altar in front of the veil that is near the Ark of the testimony, in front of the mercy seat that is over the Ark of the testimony, where I will meet with you. Aaron shall burn fragrant incense on

it; he shall burn it every morning when he trims the lamps. When Aaron trims the lamps at twilight; he shall burn incense. There shall be perpetual incense before the Lord throughout your generations.

> Exodus 30:6–8

The offering of the incense was associated with the prayers of the congregation being offered up to God. We see this clearly in Luke chapter 1 as it describes Zacharias, the father of John the Baptist, standing in his role to minister in the temple. It was his turn, as determined by lot, to offer the incense on the altar. Verse 10 tells us that "the whole multitude were in prayer outside at the hour of the incense offering," no doubt a custom carried down since Old Testament times. We see this theme referred to again in Revelation chapter 8:

> Another angel came and stood at the altar, holding a golden censer; and much incense was given to him, so that he might add it to the prayers of all the saints on the Golden altar which was before the throne. And the smoke of the incense, with the prayers of the saints, went up before God out of the angel's hand.
>
> Revelation 8:3–4

There is great symbolism in the fact that the incense was burned in fire with coals off the great altar in the main court of the tabernacle. The prayers offered up here are seasoned with the incense of praise and worship, but they are also burned with the fire of self-sacrifice that already has taken place on the great altar. Just as the incense was not allowed to be offered in any manner other than what was described in the Torah, so our prayers must conform to the Lord's prayer and be in submission to God's will. In Exodus chapter 30 after we are told how that the priests were to offer the incense on altar, we are also told that there should be no "strange" incense offered. However, Leviticus 10:1–2 tells the story of Moses's sons Nadab and Abihu who did so and God sent fire from heaven and consumed them. Again, we see that coming into God's presence, praise, worship, and prayer are not matters to be taken lightly.

"Do not lead us into temptation, but deliver us from evil" brings us to the very heart of our prayer life. We desire to be free from the temptations and the traps Satan has set for us and avoid every evil entanglement. Jesus's defeat of Satan's temptations in Luke chapter 4 gives us a picture of how to overcome our enemy through use of and application of God's word. We speak it, and He enforces it according to Matthew 16:19 and Mark 11:23–24:

> I will give you the keys to the kingdom of heaven; and whatever you bind on earth shall have been bound in heaven, and whatever you loose on earth shall have been loosed in heaven.

> Truly I say to you, whoever says to this mountain, "Be taken up and cast in the sea," does not doubt in his heart, but believes that what he says is going to happen, it will be granted him. Therefore I say to you, all things for which you pray and ask, believe that you receive them, and they will be granted you.

This battle against temptation and the devices of the enemy is at the heart of our personal spiritual warfare. The apostle Paul says in Romans chapter 7:

> I find then the principle that evil is present in me, the one who wants to do good. For I joyfully concur with the law God in the inner man, but I see a different law in the members of my body, waging war against the law my mind and making me a prisoner of the law of sin which is in my members.
>
> Romans 7:21–23

Here once again we see that we must have "boldness and confident access" to approach God's throne. As Jesus was about to raise Lazarus from the grave, he prayed these words:

> Father, I thank You that You have heard me. I knew that You always hear Me; but because of the people standing around I said it, so that they may believe that You sent Me.
>
> John 11:41–42

We must come to the point that, like Jesus, we can offer up our prayers with praise and thanksgiving. We must be fully persuaded, without any doubting, that God has heard and will answer those prayers. He has given us a promise that we have received our request at that moment.

Prayer for worship at the altar of incense:

"Lead me not into temptation but deliver me from evil" is my prayer today so that I can avoid the snares of the enemy and follow you more closely. I thank you that you hear my prayers. I submit my will to yours, and I worship you for all you have done and continue to do in my life. I lift my petitions to you for _____, and I believe that I have received. In Jesus's name, amen.

Life challenge:

Each of us has a unique set of core issues and struggles that represent the very heart of our prayer life and conversation with our Heavenly Father. Our prayers, however, will be hindered by such things as: bitterness, malice, lack of forgiveness, and unconfessed sin. Which of these most often serve as road blocks for your prayers?

FOR THINE IS THE KINGDOM

Having completed the ministry at the altar of incense, the high priest would enter the holy of holies. This chamber represents the third of the three natures of man: the eternal nature or the spirit of man. This is the place where the Holy Spirit dwells once we have received Jesus Christ as our Savior. The ministry in the holy of holies was done only once a year on the Day of Atonement.

> He shall make atonement for the holy place, because of the impurities of the sons of Israel and because of their transgressions in regard to all their sins… This shall be a permanent statute for you: in the seventh month, on the tenth day of the month, you shall humble your souls and do no work, whether the native, or the alien who sojourns among you; for it is on this day that atonement shall be made for you to cleanse you; you shall be clean from all your

sins before the Lord…Now you shall have this as a permanent statute, to make atonement for the sins of Israel for all their sins once every year.

Leviticus 16:16, 29–30, 34

The veil separating the holy of holies from the holy place had no door or opening in it. The high priest had to get on his knees and crawl under the veil to enter the most holy. This represented the complete contrition with which he had to come and minister before the ark of the covenant. It was here that the manifest presence of God dwelt in the tabernacle. There was in fact no light in the holy of holies other than the power and presence of God. The high priest would have bells on the fringe of his robe and a rope around his ankle. This was a contingency in case the sacrifice or his approach was not pleasing to God. In this case, he would be killed upon entering the holy of holies, and since none of the other priests were allowed to enter this place, the rope would be used to drag his lifeless body out into the outer chamber. The good news for us as believers in Jesus Christ is that we have his robe of righteousness to cloak our fallen humanness, and therefore, we are guaranteed the bold and confident access that the Scriptures promise us. The book of Matthew tells us that when Jesus died on the cross:

> Behold, the veil of the temple was torn in two from top to bottom; and the Earth shook and the rocks were split.
>
> Matthew 27:51

This signifies the opening of the way for all to approach to the presence of God, not just the high priest once a year, but every believer continually having access. Hebrews 10:19 says:

Therefore brethren, we have confidence to enter the holy place by the blood of Jesus. The high priest also carried a censer of fire and incense from the altar of incense which he carried before him. This also shows us that even in the holy of holies the incense of praise and worship was mixed with everything that was carried out in service to God.

> He shall take a firepan of coals of fire from upon the altar before the Lord and two handfuls of finely ground sweet incense, and bring it inside the veil. He shall put the incense on the fire before the Lord, that the cloud of incense may cover the mercy seat that is on the ark of the testimony, otherwise he will die.
>
> Leviticus 16:12–13

The ark of the covenant was the ultimate place of worship in the tabernacle. The cover of the ark of the covenant was called the mercy seat. The Hebrew word *kapporeth* used to describe this mercy seat actually means atonement. It was here that the yearly offering of blood was placed by the high priest to atone for the sins of the people. Here was the place where the manifest presence of God Almighty perpetually dwelled and provided a portal for the high priest to have interaction with the Lord.

> You shall put the mercy seat on top of the Ark, in the Ark you shall have the testimony which I shall give to you. There I shall meet with you; and from above the mercy seat, from between the two cherubim which are upon the Ark of the testimony, I will speak to you about all that I will give you in commandments for the sons of Israel.
>
> Exodus 25:21–22

Inside the ark of the covenant were the covenant pieces. These were the stone tablets Moses brought down from Mount Sinai containing the law, which represented God's guidance; the almond wood rod belonging to Aaron, which had budded, symbolizing God's authority; and a golden pot of manna, which symbolized God's provision. These covenant pieces not only stand as symbols of the covenant that was made with the people of Israel, but they also are symbols foreshadowing the new covenant that we have been made participants in. Jesus showed us this in Matthew 26:27 when He gave His disciples the cup we now recognize as the communion cup and said,

> Drink from it, all of you; for this is My blood of the covenant, which is poured out for many for the forgiveness of sins.
>
> Matthew 26:27

Hebrews chapter 12 reiterates this principle when it says,

> Jesus, the mediator of a new covenant, and to the sprinkled blood.
>
> Hebrews 12:24

Here the writer actually alludes to the sprinkling of the blood on the mercy seat and connects it with Jesus's shed blood on the cross, concretely establishing our connection to the tabernacle worship in the holy of holies. Like the high priest in the Old Testament tabernacle system, we can enter this ultimate place of worship and communion with God through the blood of Jesus and our faith in him. Jesus brings this home in most striking fashion when he says in John chapter 15,

> I am the true vine, and My Father is the vine dresser...Abide in Me, and I in you. As the branch cannot bear fruit of itself unless it abides in the vine, so neither can you unless you abide in Me. I am the vine, you are the branches; he who abides in Me and I in him, he bears much fruit, for apart from Me you can do nothing...If you abide in Me and My words abide in you, ask whatever you wish, and it will be done for you.
>
> John 15:1, 4–5, 7

Notice the repeated use of the word *abide* in these passages. This was the Greek word *meno*, which means (and is translated) to dwell, abide, continue, remain, or endure. You can see from these alternate translations that this word is rich in meaning for us in our communion with God in the holy of holies. Our entering in to the holy of holies is to be the basis of an ongoing, intimate relationship with the Lord. In fact, Psalm 91 gives us a picture of this principle in terms that are reminiscent of Sukkot, the Feast of Booths.

> He who dwells in the shelter of the Most High will abide in the shadow of the Almighty.
>
> Psalm 91:1

In this fall festival, men built wooden booths outside their homes and lived in them for seven days. This Hebrew festival, which is also called, significantly, Tabernacles, represented man dwelling with God. Notice the words *dwells* and *abides*. It is no coincidence that the passage here uses the Hebrew synonyms for the Greek word *meno*. As we saw in John 15:7, Jesus promises us that if we abide in him, whatever we wish (ask) it will be done for us. This points out to us the incredible benefits of abiding in his presence in the holy of holies. If we can come to this point on an ongoing basis, it will open the door for us to reach an incredible level of unity with the will and purposes of God. All we pray and ask for will be in keeping with His will and purposes and will be granted to us. Let us enter into this place!

Prayer for entering in the holy of holies:

Heavenly Father, give me the faith, commitment, and humility to press into the holy of holies. I recognize that only through the blood of Jesus do I have access to your presence, your favor, and your covenants. I come into your holy presence with praise and worship as Jesus taught us: "For Yours is the kingdom and the power and the glory forever." Your word says that if I abide in Christ, all my petitions will be granted, but I come now in adoration, seeking your face and not your hands. I pray according to 2 Corinthians 3:18 that I will be changed by beholding your glory into the same image—the image of Christ. In Jesus's name, amen.

Life challenge:

Now that we have gone through all the steps in the Lord's Prayer and the tabernacle worship system, are you willing to let him change, heal, and fix the issues brought to light in the other life challenges? What is the single biggest hurdle to your pursuing him fully?

Building the Tabernacle

The Lord's Prayer teaches us to pray our way through the tabernacle and into the holy of holies from the outside in. We need to realize, however, that the tabernacle was actually built from inside out. We see a detailed description of this in Exodus chapter 40.

> Moses erected the tabernacle and laid its sockets, and set up its boards, and inserted its bars and erected its pillars. He spread the tent over the tabernacle and put the covering of the tent on top of it, just as the Lord commanded Moses. Then he took the testimony and put it into the Ark, and attached the poles to the Ark, and put the Ark seat on top of the Ark. He brought the Ark into the tabernacle, and set up a veil for the screen, and screened off the Ark of the Testimony just as the Lord had commanded Moses. Then he put the table in the tent of meeting

on the north side of the tabernacle, outside the veil. He set the arrangement of bread in order on it before the Lord, just as the Lord had commanded Moses. Then he placed the lampstand in the tent of meeting, opposite the table, on the south side of the tabernacle. He lighted the lamp before the Lord, just as the Lord commanded Moses. Then he placed the gold altar in the tent of meeting in front of the veil; and he burned incense on it, just as the Lord had commanded Moses. Then he set up the veil for the doorway of the tabernacle. He set the altar of burnt offering before the doorway of the tabernacle of the tent of meeting, and offered on it the burnt offering and meal offering, just as the Lord commanded Moses. He placed the laver before the tent of meeting and the altar and put water in it for washing. From it Moses and Aaron and his sons washed their hands and their feet. When they entered the tent of meeting, and when they approached, the altar, they washed just as the Lord commanded Moses. He erected the court all around the tabernacle and the altar, and hung up the veil for the gateway of the court. Thus Moses finished the work. Then the cloud covered the tent of meeting and the glory of the Lord filled the tabernacle.

Exodus 40:18–34

First, the tent of meeting was built. The erection of the tent, which housed both the holy of holies and the holy place is symbolic of our inner nature, our mind, our will, and our emotions. Notice that when it is first set up it is empty, just as we are empty and spiritually dead before salvation. The ark of the covenant is then placed inside and the veil is hung, separating the holy of holies from the rest of the holy place. This represents the moment of salvation and the sealing of our spirit man. This is a mystery to us, but Scripture addresses this division:

> For the word of God is living and active and sharper than any two-edged sword, and piercing as far as the division of soul and spirit, of both joints and marrow, and able to judge the thoughts and intentions of the heart.
>
> Hebrews 4:12

This division also speaks to the fact that even though salvation is a spiritual transaction, it is initiated, on our part, by an act of our will in our inner nature. This act brings us to salvation. Our dead human spirits are resurrected, and we receive the indwelling of the Holy Spirit in our holy of holies or eternal nature. Then, as new believers in Christ, we begin to read and study his Word (the table of bread), pray (the altar of incense), and experience the presence of the Holy Spirit (the menorah). These spiritual disciplines begin a process the scriptures call the renewing of our minds (our holy place). This transformation produces attitudes, actions, and thought processes that are in line with the Spirit's character and contrary to our fallen internal nature. These are called in Galatians 5:22–23 the fruit of the Holy Spirit.

Finally, the cleansing of the sins of the flesh or the external nature (at the laver) together with the sacrifice of self and self-will (on the altar) combine to bring about further changes to the transformation of our lives. This final surrender of self culminates in what the scripture calls the baptism of the Holy Spirit, resulting in dramatic life change and empowerment. In fact, Jesus told His disciples not to leave Jerusalem (to begin their ministry) without the "gift of the Holy Spirit."

These milestones in our spiritual journey are supremely important to us. The tabernacle was only filled with the Shekinah glory of God when it was completed, and Aaron and his sons had washed and sanctified themselves. In the same way, we are only able to pray our way in as far as we have built our way out and prepared ourselves for entrance into the deeper places of fellowship with God.

Prayers of building the tabernacle.

Prayer for salvation:

Heavenly Father, I come to you today, acknowledging the fact that I have lived my life independent of you. I have fallen far short of your standards, which the Bible calls sin. I repent and turn from my sin and ask for your forgiveness. I know that your Son Jesus died for my sins and was resurrected. I believe on him and ask him to be my Savior and Lord. I thank you for your free gift of salvation. In Jesus's name, amen.

Prayer for the fruit of the Spirit:

Father, I know that your ways are as far above my ways as the heavens are above the earth. I need your help to change and become more like Christ in my thoughts, attitudes, and actions. Transform me by your Holy Spirit and produce in me the spiritual fruit of love, joy, peace, patience, kindness, goodness, faithfulness, gentleness, and self-control. Make all my life a testimony of your power to change. In Jesus's name, amen.

Prayer for the baptism of the Spirit:

Heavenly Father, I come to you laying self and self-will on the altar of sacrifice and submitting myself to the washing of the water of your word. By an act of my will, I crucify the flesh, I empty myself of me, and I ask you to fill me and baptize me in your Holy Spirit. I believe I receive according to Mark chapter 11, and I thank you for the gift of the Holy Spirit. In Jesus's name, amen.

Into His Gates

As the preceding chapters have pointed out repeatedly, this is a journey; one that will continue as long as the Lord leaves us on this planet. To make this journey, we have to make a beginning. An ancient proverb says, "The journey of a thousand miles begins with one step." This trip is not a thousand miles; it is much longer. It is from this world into the next and eternity. We simply have to begin. In 2 Chronicles chapter 6, King Solomon prays a prayer to dedicate the newly completed temple in Jerusalem. He invites God to enter and take up His dwelling climaxing with the following phrase:

> Therefore arise, O LORD God, to Your resting place.
> 2 Chronicles 6:41

The result?

> Now when Solomon had finished praying, fire came down from heaven and consumed the burnt offering

and the sacrifices, and the glory of the LORD filled the house.

2 Chronicles 7:1

We now know the pattern and the power of the Lord's Prayer; we need only to put it into practice in our lives. Let us pray!

Prayer of dedication and consecration:

Heavenly Father, I dedicate myself to the pursuit of your presence and life-changing power. I consecrate myself to you. Make me an instrument suitable for your service. Remove from me everything that is not in line with your will and plans. Create in me every ability, gift, and talent needed to accomplish your eternal purposes in my life. I surrender myself to you. In Jesus's name, amen.

Appendix A

The following is a compilation of the prayers in this book. This is done to allow the reader to go through them in a unified and seamless manner as they use the prayer principles taught here. These are no "formula" just a template. Your own problems, prayers, and petitions need to be molded into them.

Prayer for entrance into the tabernacle:

"Our Father who is in heaven, hallowed be Your name." I enter the tabernacle of your presence with thankfulness. Thank you for Your many and great blessings. Thank you for Your free gift of salvation in your son, Jesus Christ. For all your supply and blessings, which were accomplished and provided by the finished work of the cross, I thank you and I praise you. I magnify and declare holy your great name, for you are worthy of all worship and honor and glory and power and blessing and praise forever. In Jesus's name, amen.

Prayer for cleansing at the laver:

Heavenly Father, your kingdom come in my life, in my will, in my attitudes, and in my behavior. Cleanse me of all sins, worldly distractions, and thoughts patterns. Create in me a clean heart and a mind centered on you alone as I come into this time of prayer and fellowship with you. Sanctify me as a vessel fit for your service and worship. In Jesus's name, amen.

Prayer for cleansing at the altar:

Father, "Your will be done" in every part of my life, my thought processes, my attitudes, and my Christian walk. Right now, by an act of my will, I lay myself on your altar as a living sacrifice. I crucify my flesh according to Galatians 2:20 that no longer will it be me that lives, but Christ who lives in me. I put myself in submission to your will and in obedience to your word so that I can worship you and serve others. Prepare me to enter into your holy place. In Jesus's name, amen.

Prayer for abiding at the table of bread:

Lord, give me this day my daily bread, the bread of life that proceeds only from you. Help me to be in a perpetual state of prayer and meditation on you and Your word. Create in me a thankful heart that is always set on praising and worshipping you. Change me in your glorious presence. In Jesus's name, amen.

Prayer for standing before the menorah:

Father God, I come to you with open arms and heart. I stand before the light of your word and invite you to search me and try me. Show me the areas of my life, attitudes, actions, and thought processes that don't meet your standard. Forgive me my debts, my sins against you. Give me strength so that I, by an act of my will, can give forgiveness. Purge out of me everything that hinders our fellowship so that Your light can shine through me more clearly in a dark and fallen world. In Jesus's name, amen.

Prayer for worship at the altar of incense:

"Lead me not into temptation but deliver me from evil" is my prayer today so that I can avoid the snares of the enemy and follow you more closely. I thank you that you hear my prayers. I submit my will to yours, and I worship you for all you have done and continue to do in my life. I lift my petitions to you for _____, and I believe that I have received. In Jesus's name, amen.

Prayer for entering in the holy of holies:

Heavenly Father, give me the faith, commitment, and humility to press in to the holy of holies. I recognize that only through the blood of Jesus do I have access to your presence, your favor, and your covenants. I come into your holy presence with praise and worship as Jesus taught us: "For Yours is the kingdom and the power and the glory forever." Your word says that if I abide in Christ all my petitions will be granted, but I come now in adoration, seeking your face and not your hands. I pray according to 2 Corinthians 3:18 that I will be changed by beholding your glory into the same image, the image of Christ. In Jesus's name, amen.

Prayers of building the tabernacle.

Prayer for salvation:

Heavenly Father, I come to you today, acknowledging the fact that I have lived my life independent of you. I have fallen far short of your standards, which the Bible calls sin. I repent and turn from my sin and ask for your forgiveness. I know that your son, Jesus, died for my sins and was resurrected. I believe on Him and ask Him to be my savior and Lord. I thank you for your free gift of salvation. In Jesus's name, amen.

Prayer for the fruit of the Spirit:

Father I know that Your ways are as far above my ways as the heavens are above the earth. I need Your help to change and become more like Christ in my thoughts, attitudes, and actions. Transform me by your Holy Spirit and produce in me the spiritual fruit of love, joy, peace, patience, kindness, goodness, faithfulness, gentleness, and self-control. Make all my life a testimony of your power to change. In Jesus's name, amen.

Prayer for the baptism of the Spirit:

Heavenly Father, I come to you laying self and self-will on the altar of sacrifice and submitting myself to the washing of the water of your word. By an act of my will, I crucify the flesh, I empty myself of me, and I ask you to fill me and baptize me in your Holy Spirit. I believe I receive according to Mark chapter 11, and I thank you for the gift of the Holy Spirit. In Jesus's name, amen.

Prayer of dedication and consecration:

Heavenly Father, I dedicate myself to the pursuit of your presence and life-changing power. I consecrate myself to you.

Make me an instrument suitable for your service. Remove from me everything that is not in line with your will and plans. Create in me every ability, gift, and talent needed to accomplish your eternal purposes in my life. I surrender myself to you. In Jesus's name, amen.

Appendix B

For the reader's convenience, the following is a compilation of the seven life challenges.

It is important to enter his presence in this close personal way—free from distractions. What do you need to lay aside as you come into his courts? What mental tapes, playing in your head, that keep you from concentrating on him, do you need to turn off?

Just as ceremonial physical cleansing was an important step in tabernacle worship, mental and emotional cleansing is crucial for us as we enter in. What worldly or even ungodly thoughts and thought patterns do you need to let him cleanse as you come into his presence?

Throughout the New Testament we are taught to live a crucified life, a life that places self and self-will on the altar of sacrifice to his will. What areas of your life do you struggle with submitting to him? When is the temptation greatest for self to "crawl off the altar" and retake control of your life?

The spiritual disciplines of Bible reading/study, prayer, and communion with God are all vitally important in the life of a believer. In which of these areas do you sense God pointing out to you a deficiency in your daily walk?

As believers we are spiritually illuminated by the Holy Spirit living within us. However, it is also fundamental to our Christian walk to exhibit the fruit of the Spirit and to operate in the power of the Holy Spirit. Which of the fruits of the Spirit listed in Galatians 5:22-23 do you demonstrate the most? The least? Do you pray regularly (or ever) for the filling and empowerment of the Holy Spirit?

Each of us has a unique set of core issues and struggles that represent the very heart of our prayer life and conversation with our Heavenly Father. Our prayers, however, will be hindered by such things as bitterness, malice, lack of forgiveness, and unconfessed sin. Which of these most often serve as road blocks for your prayers?

Now that we have gone through all the steps in the Lord's Prayer and the tabernacle worship system, are you willing to let him change, heal, and fix the issues brought to light in the other life challenges? What is the single biggest hurdle to your pursuing him fully?

www.ingramcontent.com/pod-product-compliance
Lightning Source LLC
Chambersburg PA
CBHW070546300426
44113CB00011B/1810